Do Doodlebugs DOODLE?

Amazing Insect Facts

PERSNICKETY PRESS

Designed by Patricia Mitter

Library of Congress Cataloging-in-Publication Data available.

ISBN: 978-1-943978-35-9

Manufactured in China

10 9 8 7 6 5 4 3 2 1

PERSNICKETY PRESS

Produced by Persnickety Press
120A North Salem Street
Apex, NC 27502
www.Persnickety-Press.com

cpsia tracking label information
Production Location: Everbest Printing,
Guangdong, China
Production Date: 12/15/2017
Cohort: Batch No. 80566

Do Doodlebugs DOODLE?

Amazing Insect Facts

By Corinne Demas
and Artemis Roehrig
Illustrated by Ellen Shi

For Morgan, Devon, Ariadne, and Demetria,
and all other budding entomologists.
— C.D. & A.R.

For those who are scared of insects. The more
you understand, the less scary they'll become.
— E.S.

Do dragonflies breathe fire?

No! But they have a long toothed jaw and a flap at the front of their mouth that can shoot forward to catch prey.

Do water boatmen wear life jackets?

No! But they carry an air bubble under their wings and use the oxygen when they swim underwater.

Do horseflies gallop?

No! But they are the fastest flying insect on earth and can zoom much faster than a galloping horse.

Do robber flies rob banks?

No! But they use their keen eyesight to ambush and catch their dinner. Their saliva paralyzes the prey and turns the insides to juice so the robber fly can suck it out.

Do fireflies roast marshmallows?

No! But some of them blink the yellow or red light on their abdomens to attract mates. Different species flash different patterns.

Do stink bugs take baths?

No! They like to be stinky because that discourages predators from eating them. The smell comes from glands in their abdomens.

Do yellow jackets wear yellow jackets?

No! But their bright coloring warns other animals they are venomous. Birds beware!

Do booklice have library cards?

No! But they sometimes eat the paste used to hold book bindings together. They also eat algae and lichen on trees.

Do kissing bugs send valentines?

No! But they love to bite people (and dogs, too) around the mouth and eyes.

Do bed bugs wear pajamas?

No! But even without pajamas they can survive when it's really cold by lowering the freezing point of the fluids in their bodies.

Do doodlebugs doodle?

YES!!!

Doodlebugs, the larvae of antlions, leave spiraling, winding trails in the sand that look like doodles.

Photo by: Matthew Roehrig

WHAT IS AN INSECT?

Insects have been on the earth for 400 million years, while humans have been around for fewer than two million. About 90% of all the animals on earth are insects. There are probably more than five million species of insects, but only about a million are named so far, and new species are being discovered every day. Perhaps someday **YOU** could be the one to choose a funny name for an insect!

Entomologists, scientists who study insects, group them into different categories (orders or families), such as beetles, flies, or bugs. So not all insects are bugs! All insects have three major body parts: a head, a thorax, and an abdomen. They all have six legs, and most have one or two sets of wings. Insects are invertebrates (they don't have backbones). They have exoskeletons (their skeleton is on the outside of their body) and are cold-blooded. They breathe through holes along their abdomen and thorax, called spiracles.

photo by Ondrej Prosicky/Shutterstock.com

DRAGONFLIES

(Order: Odonata)

While dragonflies may look scary, they don't sting or bite humans. They have been around on earth for 300 million years, since before the time of the dinosaurs. There are over 3,000 species of dragonflies. The largest species has a wingspan of over seven inches. The adults eat other insects, and the larvae, which live in the water, may also eat tadpoles or small fish.

Photo by BM/Shutterstock.com

WATER BOATMEN

(Family: Corixidae)

Water boatmen are a type of true bug. There are 120 different species. Water boatmen eat mainly algae. Some things that eat water boatmen are: birds, frogs, dragonflies, and even humans! People collect water boatmen eggs, which are laid on plants in the water, and turn the eggs into a kind of flour to cook with.

Photo by Anatolich/Shutterstock.com

HORSEFLIES

(Family: Tabanidae)

Horseflies have been around since the late Jurassic period, so there is a chance they might have bitten dinosaurs! Horseflies eat nectar and other plant matter. Only female horseflies bite animals (and humans). They need the extra protein from blood so they can lay eggs. The main predators of adult horseflies are birds.

ROBBER FLIES
(Family: Asilidae)

There are about one thousand species of robber flies, which are true flies, and they vary a lot in appearance. They eat mostly other insects—even wasps and bees! They usually catch their prey in flight. Their larvae live in the ground and eat small invertebrates or eggs.

FIREFLIES
(Family: Lampyridae)

Fireflies, also called lightning bugs, aren't either flies or bugs—they are actually a type of beetle. There are over 2,000 different species of fireflies. In some species, only the male can fly. Fireflies have a bad taste, and some species are even poisonous. Firefly lights are created using bioluminescence, a chemical reaction. Their diets vary depending on the species, and some don't eat at all as adults. The larvae are predatory, and some eat things like snails and slugs.

STINK BUGS
(Family: Pentatomidae)

Stink bugs are a type of true bug. While there are other insects that also stink, most stinky insects are, in fact, stink bugs. They can be big pests to farmers. Their main predators are birds, who don't seem to mind the stink, and other insects and spiders, who eat their eggs.

YELLOW JACKETS
(Family: Vespidae)

Although they look a lot like bees, yellow jackets are actually a type of wasp, closely related to hornets. They can sting multiple times, but sometimes lose their stinger. They live in colonies with queens, workers, and males. A single colony may have as many as 5,000 workers. While the workers eat mostly nectar and sap, they also collect meat and fruit to feed the larvae in the colony, which is why they might go after your lunch!

BOOKLICE
(Family: Liposcelidae)

Booklice are currently thought to be relatives of head lice, the kind that might hide out in your hair. While you may find booklice among books or slightly moldy paper, their more natural habitat is under decaying tree bark. They have very tiny wings, or no wings at all, depending on the species.

KISSING BUGS
(Family: Triatominae)

Kissing bugs, also known as assassin bugs, are infamous for causing the spread of Chagas disease in humans and dogs. This disease is actually very hard to catch, because an infected bug would need to bite you and then deposit its feces into the bite. They are a type of true bug. Most species of kissing bugs make up their diet from the blood of vertebrates (animals with backbones) and are nocturnal, which is why they're sometimes called vampire bugs.

BED BUGS
(Family: Cimicidae)

Bed bugs are true bugs, and are parasites who eat only blood. There are about seventy-four different species, which parasitize different animals, for instance some species feed on bats, others on birds, and others on humans! They may double or triple their body size while they eat.

DOODLEBUGS
(Family: Myrmeliontidae)

If you don't like ants, you'll love doodlebugs! Doodlebugs are also known as antlions, since their larvae hunt ants. The larvae make doodle-paths in the sand while they are looking for a perfect place to build their trap. When an ant comes along, the doodlebug flicks sand at it, causing it to fall into the funnel-shaped trap. Then they grab and eat it. Doodlebugs grow up to look a little like dragonflies as adults, but unlike dragonflies, they're nocturnal, and they're not great fliers.

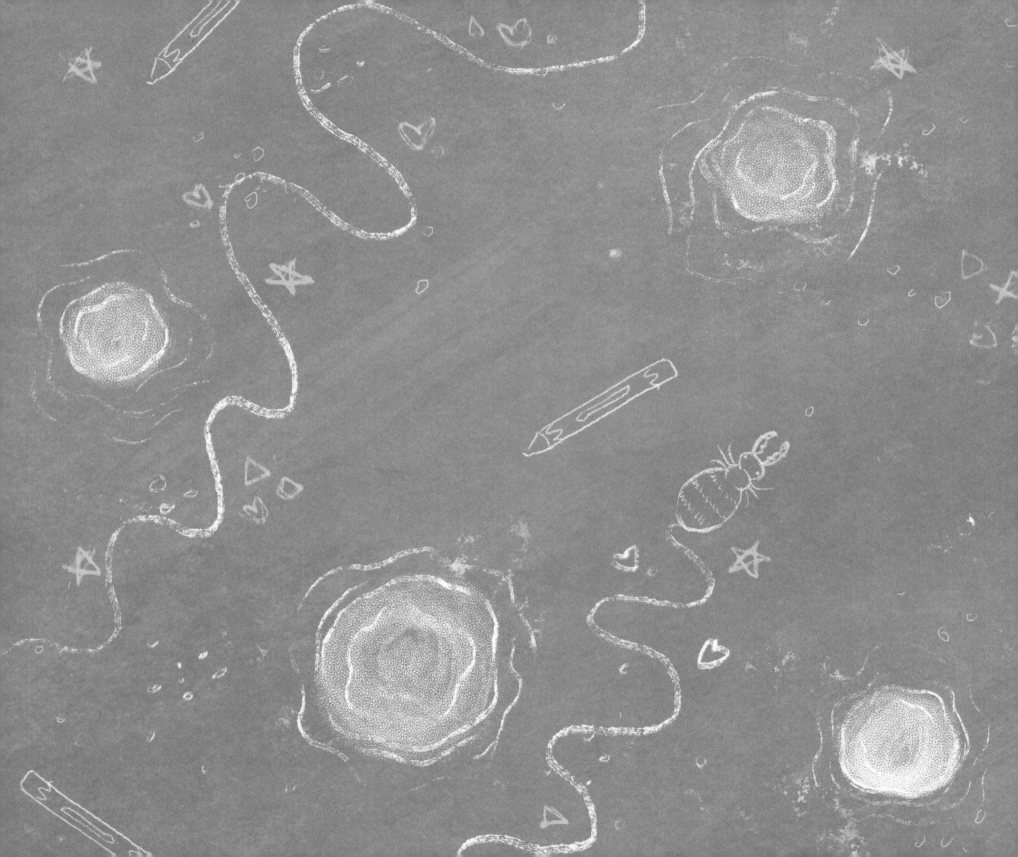